NEW YORK REVIEW BOOK
POETS

MARINA TSVETAEVA
a classicist and whose motl
Moscow and published her .
She left Russia in 1922 with her two children and her husband, Sergei Efron, who fought against the Red Army in the 1918–1921 Civil War but was later to become a Soviet spy. Often living from hand to mouth, the family remained abroad until 1939. Two years later, after the execution of her husband and the arrest of her daughter, Tsvetaeva committed suicide. *Earthly Signs*, a selection of the diaries she kept in Moscow between 1917 and 1922, is published by NYRB Classics.

ANDREW DAVIS is a poet, cabinetmaker, and visual artist. His translation of Osip Mandelstam's *Voronezh Notebooks* is published by NYRB Poets; his current project is the long poem *IMPLUVIUM*. He divides his time between Santa Fe, New Mexico, and the north coast of Spain.

Marina Tsvetaeva

Three by Tsvetaeva

TRANSLATED FROM THE RUSSIAN
BY ANDREW DAVIS

NYRB/POETS

 NEW YORK REVIEW BOOKS   *New York*

THIS IS A NEW YORK REVIEW BOOK
PUBLISHED BY THE NEW YORK REVIEW OF BOOKS
207 East 32nd Street, New York, NY 10016
www.nyrb.com

Library of Congress Cataloging-in-Publication Data
Names: T͡Svetaeva, Marina, 1892–1941, author. | Davis, Andrew,
   translator, writer of introduction.
Title: Three by Tsvetaeva / by Marina Tsvetaeva, translation and
   introduction: Andrew Davis.
Identifiers: LCCN 2023050121 (print) | LCCN 2023050122 (ebook)
   | ISBN 9781681378329 (paperback) | ISBN 9781681378336 (ebook)
Subjects: LCSH: T͡Svetaeva, Marina, 1892–1941—Translations into
   English. | LCGFT: Poetry.
Classification: LCC PG3476.T75 T48 2024 (print) | LCC PG3476.T75 (ebook)
   | DDC 891.71/42—dc23/eng/20231026
LC record available at https://lccn.loc.gov/2023050121
LC ebook record available at https://lccn.loc.gov/2023050122

ISBN 978-1-68137-832-9
Available as an electronic book; ISBN 978-1-68137-833-6

Cover and book design by Emily Singer

Printed in the United States of America on acid-free paper.
10 9 8 7 6 5 4 3 2 1

Contents

INTRODUCTION

EVENTS OF THE PAST, in their immutability and their distance from us, acquire solidity, an aura of inevitability. And fair enough: hard to argue with the authority of "having happened." There was an extraordinary bloom of poetry in Russian in the first decades of the twentieth century. It happened. But Osip Mandelstam, Anna Akhmatova, Boris Pasternak, Marina Tsvetaeva: What *was* it that produced such a remarkable generation?

A devotion to language instead of propaganda? To the person above the collective? Individual authority over obedience? But isn't this the stock in trade of any poet? In this case it was an intrinsic, unquestioned, inexplicable conviction of individual authority and responsibility, precisely at the moment of radical social dissolution and uncertainty, and in the face of an irresistible movement toward conformity and absolutism. It was as if, under the force of events, and only for a moment, a crack in history opened, and through it gushed an elemental lava, the word and the world's own truth, a truth that could only be expressed through the conduit of the individual voice. Which gives a suggestion of the strange and contradictory forces that were in play in the revolutionary period, and the bitterness of the success of the October Revolution and its aftermath.

Even in a moment of history distinguished by the ubiquity and intensity of individual suffering, the facts of Marina Tsvetaeva's life still elicit a particular horror. If only she had been slightly more compromising, if only she had been slightly less devoted to her son and husband, both manifestly unworthy of her loyalty, she might have avoided the worst of what occurred! But Tsvetaeva was faithful to Tsvetaeva.

Tsvetaeva was born in Moscow in 1892, and her life encompassed the period of intellectual and political turmoil in Russia which led to the revolutions of 1905 and February and October of 1917, and culminated in the Bolshevik takeover, the dictatorship of Stalin, and the disasters of World War II. Her father was a professor of art, her mother a frustrated concert pianist. They must have found the young Marina a trial. Headstrong, intractable, passionate, she was an indifferent student and even less willing musician. A long stay in Europe in her adolescence with her mother, who was being treated for her ultimately fatal tuberculosis, seemed to leave little mark. Like most of her contemporaries she was affected by the revolutionary fervor of the times, but her response was idiosyncratic and personal, and she early manifested her two central, lifelong preoccupations: poetry, and an uninterrupted chain of intense romantic relationships with members of both sexes. Her first published book of poetry, *The Evening Album* (1910), was met with great approval and appreciation for her precocious talents, but also some bemusement at what was seen as her petulant clinging to the language of childhood and adolescence.

Her marriage to Sergei Efron at the age of twenty produced two daughters, Ariadna and Irina. In the aftermath of the October Revolution, Sergei fled south to join the White Army. Trapped in Moscow alone with her children and in the midst of the terrible privations of the period, Tsvetaeva was forced to entrust her second child, Irina, to the care of a state orphanage. There Irina died of starvation in 1920. Extraordinarily, this period of poverty and extreme emotional distress between the October Revolution and Tsvetaeva's emigration was enormously productive poetically. Among the works produced were her fragmentary memoir of the period, *Earthly Signs* (published by NYRB Classics), the two books of poetry *Mileposts II* and *Craft*, and a collection of poems about the February and October Revolutions called *The Demesne of the Swans*.

In 1921 she received word that Sergei, who had been evacuated with the remnants of the White Army from the Crimea, was in Prague. She immediately decided to join him. A series of affairs during their separation had done nothing to lesson her devotion to him, a loyalty that in the end would prove disastrous.

She left the Soviet Union in 1922, beginning a long exile among the Russian émigré community in Europe. There she was treated, at least initially, as one of the luminaries of Russian literature. After a period in Berlin, she began an extended stay in Prague, supported by the enlightened government of Tomáš Masaryk. Again she and Sergei were forced to live apart, and again she embarked on a series of romantic relationships, the most important of which was with Konstantin Rodzevich, the subject of her two great extended poems "Poem of the Mountain" and "Poem of the End." Her productivity during the time in Prague (1922–1925) was again extraordinary: besides the two poems listed above, among other things she produced the book-length *The Ratcatcher**—which was completed in Paris—and the last of her long poems based, like "Backstreets," on material from Russian folklore, *The Swain*.

In late 1925 she moved to Paris with her husband, daughter, and a son, Mur, born in Prague. There, despite her tenuous economic circumstances, she initially enjoyed great success and published voluminously. Her string of romantic involvements also continued unabated. During one extraordinary period she carried on a simultaneous epistolary romance with both Boris Pasternak and Rainer Maria Rilke. (See *Letters, Summer 1926: Boris Pasternak, Marina Tsvetayeva, Rainer Maria Rilke*, also published by NYRB Classics.) Eventually, however, her outspokenness and unconventionality estranged her from the Russian émigré community, which most particularly could not forgive her inability to confront the obvious and condemn her husband, rumored (it seems accurately) to have been a Soviet agent and to have had a hand in the murder of two Soviet defectors.

Her husband, daughter, and son all urged a return to the Soviet Union. After resisting their entreaties for a number of years, and despite her persistent and very prescient misgiv-

---

* *The Ratcatcher* is a version in poetry of the story generally known as "The Pied Piper of Hamelin." It is an extended example of the "political" theme that appears with regularity in Tsvetaeva's work, including in part 4 of "The Poem of the End": a searing satire of bourgeois culture. It exists in English in a marvelous translation by Angela Livingstone.

ings, she finally left Paris for Moscow on June 12, 1939. That decision would prove to be an unmitigated disaster. In 1941 both Ariadna and Sergei were arrested. Ariadna disappeared into the Gulag; Sergei was shot. Tsvetaeva and Mur were left alone, without a home and without means of support. They were saved from absolute destitution by the intervention of a few friends, among them Pasternak. With the advent of the German invasion in 1941, Tsvetaeva and Mur were evacuated to the town of Elabuga in the Tatar Republic. Abandoned, isolated, and impoverished, on August 31, 1942, she hanged herself. Mur was drafted into the Soviet army and sent to the front, where he perished.

The three poems in this collection were all written between 1922 and 1924, "Backstreets" (a title more commonly translated as "Sidestreets" in English) in Moscow and "Poem of the Mountain" and "Poem of the End" in Prague before her departure for Paris. "Poem of the Mountain" and "Poem of the End" are generally considered some of her finest poetry; "Backstreets," on the other hand, is almost unknown in English. As far as I have been able to ascertain, this is the first complete translation of the poem in that language. Published as the final poem of the larger collection *Craft*, in its day it was considered unintelligible. Despite its difficulties, in its emotional intensity and poetic pyrotechnics it is, I think, worthy to take its place among Tsvetaeva's greatest achievements.

"Poem of the Mountain" and "Poem of the End" both concern the end of her affair with Rodzevich. While many poets have written separate attempts on the same original subject, these are unusual in the length and complexity of each distinct treatment, which gives us a remarkable opportunity to appreciate the full extent of Tsvetaeva's virtuosity. To my ear, "Poem of the Mountain" is the more formal and studied of the two, based as it is to a large extent on the play between the Russian words "to speak" (*gavorit*) and "to mourn" (*garevat*), and on the elaborate and classic three-way pun in Russian between "mountain" (*gará*), "grief" (*góre*), and "to burn" (*garét*). "Poem of the End" is the greater poem, using Tsvetaeva's quintessential techniques of fractured language and neologism to incarnate emotional intensity.

"Backstreets," on the other hand, according to Tsvetaeva's own later testimony, is a retelling of the Russian epic tale (*bylina*) of Dobrynya and Marinka. This is amusing, because while the poem does contain a number of elements from that story, in other respects it goes deliriously off the rails. In the original story the hero Dobrynya is seduced by the witch Marinka and turned into an aurochs, the extinct European ancestor to modern cattle. Marinka is then forced by Dobrynya's sister (or mother), herself possessed of magic powers, to restore Dobrynya to his original form. This she does, though at the same time extorting from him a promise to marry her in exchange for the restoration. He marries her, but murders her on their wedding night. Almost none of this makes it into "Backstreets," at least in the form or sequence described in the *bylina*, though the poem does retain the story's aura of magic and menace. In fact, while her contemporaries found the poem incomprehensible (part of the reason the poem has languished in obscurity), it seems to me that a modern audience will have a much easier time recognizing in the poem, beneath everything, a remarkable description of a highly charged erotic encounter. The poem is, however, in its extraordinary complexity, an inexhaustible mine of meaning, and other readers and translators will find other aspects of the poem to emphasize.

"Poem of the Mountain" and "Poem of the End" both seem, superficially, to describe versions of the stock figure of the "woman aggrieved" or the "woman abandoned." But "aggrieved," "abandoned"—the suggestion of passivity and lack of agency implied in the passive voice is not appropriate to either poem. Something more sophisticated is at work. Tsvetaeva's sympathies, and her poetic imagination, extend beyond herself into all parts of the experience, including the person of her departing lover. And the whole event, as a consequence, radiates a richness, a kind of consequence, an air of inevitability; even, at the end, a strange hint of victory.

How does this work? Here "Backstreets" comes to our aid. Though written before the other two poems and of remarkable structural complexity, it is the clearer expression of Tsvetaeva's understanding of the nature of human love. It purports to be, as I have said, a retelling of the story of Dobrynya and Marinka, but there are a number of different voices and presences in the poem. There is a callow young man (both as himself and as a stand in for Dobrynya), a seductive woman (both as herself, as Tsvetaeva, and as a stand in for Marinka), the voice of the author herself (most often in sotto voce commentaries on the progress of the story), and, most strangely of all, the semi-personified feminine character of "azure." "Azure" seems to be both heaven and its incarnation, both paradise and its apotheosis. "She" is the endpoint of all desire but takes no active role, unless you feel, as I am tempted to, that in the end the Marinka/Tsvetaeva figure melds with "azure" to form a final figure of ecstatic transformation.

In any case, one of the things that makes the poem so difficult to read is that the "voice" of the poem jumps continually, and without warning or indication, between the various characters. This may seem nothing more than a strange, even annoying, narrative tic, but it is entirely the point. Tsvetaeva inhabits, moves among, all points of view. The poem is a theater of relationship, and Tsvetaeva embodies, successively, all the characters, male and female, moves them like puppets—including herself as narrator. The point being that love, in its essence, is not so much an action with an active and a passive party, with a perpetrator and a victim, a seducer and a seduced, as it is a play in which all participate and which, necessarily, has an end.

A play in which all participate, but with a caveat. In "Poem of the Mountain" and "Poem of the End," after all, who is it that is narrating the story? And in "Backstreets," who is it that is left transformed as an aurochs? In all three poems, it is the woman who has the final speech in the drama, the final say. And in "Backstreets," more than just the final say. Unlike the *bylina*, where a terrible retribution is visited on Marinka for her power and presumption, and unlike other stories in the Western canon, for example Circe and Odysseus, the feminine presence is in control throughout, with no sense of future masculine vengeance or reassertion of masculine power.

Which helps us understand that unexpected grace note of victory, of acceptance, at the end of the other two poems.

More than acceptance: a kind of ownership of the whole event. For Tsvetaeva, the end of an affair was not a failure of love but the expression of its very essence. Permanence and love are mutually contradictory. The end of love, like the end of life itself, is a pain that must be lived through, must be embraced. It is to be regretted, but it is how things are. It is a play of agony, but it is not a tragedy. Suffering, yes; but in no sense defeat.

—*Andrew Davis*

A NOTE ON THE TRANSLATION

MODERN RUSSIAN POETRY is as comfortable with rhyme and meter as modern English poetry is not. In fact, the great and unique virtue of that poetry—its extraordinary musicality—when brought over directly into English sounds hackneyed and stale. Marina Tsvetaeva's early poetry largely limited itself to traditional forms and traditional rhymes—at which, from the beginning, she showed herself a master. But by the time she wrote the poems collected here she had developed her remarkable capacity to write poetry that appeared to be conventional while in fact being utterly sui generis in structure, and filled with all matter of half-rhymes, suggestions of rhymes and brilliant intimations of form and rhythm, all on top of the more traditional harmonies. So, ironically, an English translation that comes, so to speak, from the opposite direction, not from structure but from lack of structure, but pays a maximum of attention to organic cadence and to an organic sense of harmony, is not a bad intimation of the original. Easier said than done!

There are, however, specific characteristics of her verse, dramatically so in the poems collected here, that must be absorbed and faithfully reproduced in any translation, both to give some sort of representation of her specific genius with language and to suggest her radical relationship to language itself. The first is her use of neologism, compound or portmanteau words that she sometimes separates with hyphens and sometimes not. The second is breaking words apart with dashes, such as *para—dise* or *mon—ey*. The third is the breaking apart of phrases and sentences themselves, also with dashes, not at "natural" and necessary points of punctuation but as if to indicate a catch of breath or a momentary break in a stream of emotion. I have tried to indicate compound words with hyphens, divided words with an em dash, and a broken phrase or sentence with an em dash set off by spaces. In some cases a single divided word in Russian has had to be replaced with a series of words in English, which I have also separated with an em dash. Further complicating matters is the fact that Tsvetaeva habitually used the dash to separate sentences and thoughts—like Emily Dickinson, it was her favorite and most characteristic form of punctuation—as well as an indication of direct speech. This promiscuous use of the dash makes it often very difficult, particularly in "The Poem of the End," to determine who is speaking, and whether "out loud" or simply in the flow of the narrative. In any case, taken together, her use of the dash and her aggregation and fracturing of words and phrases is one of the most distinctive qualities of her verse, contributing both to the unique, stuttering flow of its metrics, and to the strange and ubiquitous sensation of a language used at the limit of its possibilities.

And a note on method, and acknowledgements. My Russian is self-taught, with all the limitations that would suggest.

While this would seem to recommend a collaboration with a native speaker from the beginning, or at least the use of a literal trot, I prefer to work alone. I work until I have a presentable first draft, until my own response to the original poetry is substantially complete, aurally and poetically coherent, and sufficiently sturdy to be relatively immune to outside influence. The virtue of this approach is the virtue of a single voice—a single response to the original poetry. As well as a word-by-word experience of the language which could not be more intimate. The problem with this approach is the inevitable errors and misapprehensions encrusted in the text which need, painfully, to be pried out.

Fortunately, both with my previous translation of Osip Mandelstam's *Voronezh Notebooks* and with this translation, I have found extremely competent and sympathetic readers to help me with this task: Michael Ossorgin with Mandelstam and Kirill Velizhanin with Tsvetaeva. Michael is the son of old friends and the director of the Russian program at Fordham University, Kirill a lucky discovery. A theoretical physicist, he is as sensitive to language as he is good-natured and patient. Like Michael with the Mandelstam, Kirill had an immeasurable effect on the depth and coherence of this translation, for which I could not be more grateful. Obviously, any remaining problems are no fault of his, but only evidence of my own ignorance, or intransigence.

Finally, and most importantly, I want to thank my longtime partner Dee Homans. Without whom, nothing.

—A.D.

Three by Tsvetaeva

Backstreets

to Alexei Podgaetsky-Chabrov
in memory of our last time in Moscow

Saw nothing our young man? — have no idea!
Heard nothing our young man? — have not a clue!
In that brilliant white-rustle of the dresses
On those backstreets of Ignataev-town.

So she burns from night till light,
So performs the magic rite,
To God, she offers up a victim,
In oak-smoke sends up her petition.

But what's that jingle? — bracelet, little wrist!
But what's that murmur? — a little spell!
Try out youthful happiness
On those backstreets of Ignataev-town!

A stump. Two potholes.
Some wattle fencing, fallen.
Trackless — in darkness,
Of all those windows — number seven.

While you sit at home — consider;
At number six — one more good look:
The young fishwife at streamside darts
A lazy glance — won't take the hook?

He'll blow — he'll flush with fire,
He'll spit — he'll fork the ruble over,
Alas, my brainy handsome one,
Language — cannot venture further!

That's why the half-closed eyes, the languid looks
Along the sculpted incline of his shoulder.
They don't spend cash on empty words
On those backstreets of Ignataev-town!

But how to enter? — by a leaving.
And how to speak? — unspeak, unsay.
And cross myself? — Why should I?
And all that Christ-stuff? — tossed away.

Seek a blessing in the web-whip of the spider
Without a stumble — loud and clear!
My child, my little man discover
Your sacred precinct here.

Curtain mine — my little curtain!
My pagan-scripted scrap of lace!
A rag-a-flutter-blind-a-piercing pain!
Don't draw the curtain on my face!

Slow down, young man: no clock to beat!
No marvels, surely, hidden in these sheets!
Along the ridge the coal-black pigeons
Softly bill and coo, in search of love:

>About white shoulders,
>Don't brush them aside,
>About sweet minglings —
>No guilt; no sighs...

>About bliss, about flattery
>About green leaves,
>Don't chew — these morsels;
>Don't crack — these seeds...

But still, young man, don't lose your courage,
You blush-to-take-communion-from-this-cup?
They look you straight in the eye — they're anything
    but chilly
On those backstreets of Ignataev-town!

How tightly, coil on coil,
These scarves are wrapped!
She walks the streets with apples
And with rubies, with pawns and rooks.

(From my burning lips
A fevered madness comes!
From my burning lips —
The veins inside me thrum!)

With pawns and rooks, with rubies,
My mouth so sweet
It tastes just like
A mother's teat!

(My rouged-all-over one,
Chill daughter-of-the-mist.
My fevered-crazy one;
Daughter of fever-craziness!)

◆　◆　◆

Par—a—dise!
Oh—a—wave!
Pluck what's ripe!
Let's be brave!

Apple — ruby,
Apple — gold.
Before experience —
Let's be bold!

Apple — flattery,
Apple — fin.
Don't touch
That skin!

Keen-eared — deaf,
Sharp-eyed — blind;
Pigeons above you;
Pay no mind!

To the weak — the whip,
To the bold — the fin.
Don't eye the apples,
Take them in!

As if a slash for
A right hand, a splash!
No white hand but
Tail of pangolin!

As if in place of a left hand
He seized — a whip!
A maddened viper
Straight to his left eye!

Like a lash across the shoulders
He wants — to scream:
The flash of silk
A heavenly stream.

Par—a—dise!
Hea—ven — all!
Faint! — Swoon!
Snow! — Fall!

Apples — for garlic?
Won't think twice!
Heaven-daughter
Of paradise.

Little river — a ripple,
Little river — rippling,
Don't clutch the hand —
Of my darling...

Half lying broken,
Half turned turtle,
Heavenly-iridescent
Coracle

Little fish — a splash,
Little river — frail,
Of all my dear one —
Only the tail.

Just a little journey —
Pleasant to the eye!
Sails of Shamakhi
For you and I!

(What's behind such snotty foolishness:
Hiding your chestnut curls behind a shift!)

To young men, among
Rivers I am famous.
Mouthwatering, heavenly —
Nothing more delicious!

(My little whispers, my little cries,
My sweet-saliva, sweet-music of my sighs!)

As if beneath these whispers —
The soul like a jump and a howl,
As if beneath these whispers —
A head like an aurochs' horn!

(On the stern, the coal-black pigeons
Softly bill and coo, in search of love:)

Of starting ribs, of swollen gums,
Of famished spring,
Of un-combed-flax,
Un-sent-greetings.

And what's this flaxen hair to us,
Little head of green?
Your earthy greeting —
In a sea of silk:

Bow down,
Bow down!

Put the flax
To the comb,
That the son,
Waking, not say:

To Mama!
To Mama!

The river — pours
A breadth of iridescence.
You see — Mama
Is standing in a field:

Bow down,
Bow down!

And still bow down
To the east — the grasses,
This thrill
Has cost us —

No memory!
No memory!

Oh! — Lightning!
Oh! — It burns!
Not — lightning!
A horse — neighs!

One — on the legs,
Two — by the braids,
Three — song of glory.
But —

Neither braids nor fleece,
Neither rivers nor canoes,
Two reins! A driver!
Burn up the road!

Gorgeous that horse,
As if in an icon.
I am the chase,
I am the stallion.

Like a horse race
In — the — chest!
A fire — a fever!
Burn up the road!

Beneath both reins!
Run, my chestnut!
Like a lie, hidden in the chest:
Seven, even seven times
Seven and still —
Seven.
Burn up the road, driver,
Into darkness!

Darkness — behind!
No clatter of hooves!
Enflame my cheeks!
Strip my veins!

A flush in the forehead — a neigh,
A chest—nut—rein!

One kind of sweetness!
But twelve kinds of torture!
Drop the rein!
Hands open wider!

— But! — Bread of this kingdom
For centuries of days — No!

Cling,
Cling,
To the blackened
Caldron!

Don't lie: the green flax
Is not pitch-black!

Bow,
Bend down,
By your eyelashes hold on!
Beneath the deadly hiss lie down,
The hiss of tempered arrow.
Ai, flax!

Ai, faded flax,
Flax from Tsaritsyn!
The rivers of the earth preserved
A funeral prayer:

They poured out through eyelashes,
Through the eyes they poured,
Through the earth they poured,
Salty!

Through salty soils — eye sockets
Of this earth, abundant with rye.
How can it be, distinguished guests,
You so quickly — said goodbye?

A bitter soil — this little earth,
As much as you want — of salt!
Could it be, painted ladies,
You enjoyed — so little pleasure?

A little less, a little more? —
Cart provided!
Come along with me
To fiery torment!

Oh — lightning!
Oh — thunder!
Not — lightning:
To home — a stallion!

One — by a step,
Two — with a leap,
Three — sparks fly,
But:

Neither fire nor caldron,
Neither horse nor saddle,
Two wings into blue,
Into the a—
                    zure!

Azure, azure,
Steep mountain!
Azure, azure,
Second earth!

Dawn-daughter-of-Lazarus,
Blue-daughter-of-perfume,
Azure, azure,
My cool, my chill!
A—zure!

And you, left behind, this one last time,
Stand still! Draw in!
The last soft breath
Of this earth of rye:

Hills and fords, and furrows,
And all things green.
The whiff of dung, intense, strong-smelling —
My own earth!

A caldron, bottomless!
A bright-blue-palm-of-the-hand!
Azure, azure,
Blue-daughter-of-the-lake,
A—zure!

And for this last one, deserted,
For our young man — through all this blue:
At early mass, not even
A prayer for the departed...

In the forge — they beat out glory,
To the lips — they raise a toast,
For a friend — they sing of honor
To A—zure.

Azure, azure,
Stirrups of gold!
Azure, azure,
Where did you lead?

Soaring-daughter-of-a-hawk,
Rippling-daughter-of-a-rainbow,
Deep-earth-daughter-of-a-ruby:
Azure!

A ringing, a ringing-without-dreaming,
Through sound-beyond-all-sounds!
Here, little heads don't bend:
Even so we ascend!

Deep blue, smoking-censer,
Through smoke-beyond-all-smoke!
On my chest, still eleven,
Still eleven plus one!

Amen,
A prayer for the dead,
A sea-song of praise,
Blue-shroud-daughter,
But —

World-beyond-all-worlds,
A mirage — the days!
Forgotten — the world,
Forgotten — we.

Blue-you-be-praised,
Be-gone-out-to-sea!
A starry blue —
Our canopy.

But beyond all
Illusions — there!
My vestments —
Like a stair!

Deaf feather-head:
The seafloor's beyond reach,
Like a stone the cry sinks —
Is dissolved in the deep.

You started all this,
You caused all this mess:
Deep blue — to your boot tips,
Deep blue — to your head...

To fall — but not fall,
To swim — but not far.
Sate your soul
On what you are!

Sweet man, let go!
They'll refuse all that weight!
In order to accept —
One must forsake!

First sign of decay,
At the city margin!
These earths —
Are twenty-seven!

But in all these departures
Steal a quick glance!
My earths are like —
The hollow of my hand!

Sweet man, don't cling:
For there's no need:
For there's no lie:
For there's no husband,

And here there's no wife,
Or burning wounds,
But harvests without hands,
Vows without sounds.

Holding nothing back,
— Giving all! —
My wound's
Like a lark...

Toward a —

Azure, azure
Steep shoulders of perfection!
Azure, azure,
What was your intention?

Where did you lead us?
Where have you brought us?
You covered your tracks,
You hid your destination.

Toward a —

Toward azure — the destroyer,
From first aura — to aurora;
Bellow, in harness,
Under the charm!:
The vacant glance,
The furrowed brow,
The golden horn.

◆   ◆   ◆

Aurochs' track at the turning;
And from there on — nothing!

◆   ◆   ◆

Moscow
April 1922

Poem of the Mountain

Beloved, do my words surprise you?
Those who part all talk like drunks
And love a good time...

—Hölderlin

DEDICATION

Shocking, I know — but it's a mountain
Off my shoulders — and a lift to my spirits.
Let me sing of my mourning:
Of my mountain!

And I'll fill this black pit — never,
Not now, not ever.
Let me sing my mourning
From the mountaintop.

I.

That mountain was like the breast
Of a recruit, felled by a shell.
The mountain wanted virgin
Lips, the mountain demanded

A wedding celebration.
— The ocean, in a cockle,
Suddenly burst out in "Hurrah!" —
The mountain gave chase and did battle.

That mountain was like thunder!
A breast, beat on by Titans!
(That last house on the mountain —
On the way out of town — do you remember?)

That mountain was — worlds!
God charges dearly for a peaceful world!
. . . .
The mountain was the source of misery,
That mountain over the city.

2.

Not Sinai, not Parnassus,
A naked hill like a barracks —
Ready! Aim! Fire! —
Then why, to my eyes
(The time not May, but October)
Was that mountain — paradise?

3.

Like paradise, offered in my palm —
Don't touch it, it might burn!
The mountain tripped us, threw
Its rutted slopes between our legs.

As if with a Titan's great paws
And the branches of a bush —
The mountain clutched our coattails,
Commanded us: stand still!

Oh, far from your routine paradise —
Drafts on drafts on drafts!
The mountain knocked us to the ground,
It summoned us: lie down!

An attack of panic,
— What? You still don't get it! —
The mountain, like a procuress —
Here, it pointed: holiness . . .

4.

Pomegranate seed of Persephone,
How to forget you in the winter frosts?
I remember lips, like a parted shell,
Slightly opened to mine.

Persephone, ruined by a seed!
The stubborn crimson of your lips,
And your eyelashes — serrated,
And the golden tooth of a star.

5.

Not illusion — passion; not imagination!
And not deception — just evanescence!
And how, in this world, could we ever be
In love like normal people!

And when was it ever sensible or simple:
Simply — a hill, simply — a mound...
They say that by its thirst for the abyss
You take the measure of a mountain.

In the thickets of brown heather,
In the stricken islands of pine...
(Height of delirium — beyond the
Limit of life)
                    — But now, take me! Your...

But the quiet delights of the family,
The babbling of baby chicks — alas!
Because in this world we were —
Demigods of love!

6.

The mountain mourned (and mountains mourn
With caustic clay at times of parting),
The mountain mourned the pigeon
Tenderness of our simple mornings.

The mountain mourned our friendship:
The indissoluble kinship of our lips!
The mountain murmured that it only comes
To each — in proportion to their *tears*.

Still the mountain mourned, that life's —
A Gypsy camp, and all of it a market for the heart!
Still the mountain mourned: at least
He sent off Hagar — with the child!

Still it murmured, the demon spins,
And there are no set figures in the game.
The mountain murmured. We were mute.
We left it to the mountain to decide.

7.

The mountain mourned, it only ends
In sadness — what now is blood and fire.
The mountain murmured, it will not
Release us, or let you go off with another!

The mountain mourned, it only ends
In smoke — what now is World, is Rome.
The mountain murmured, we'll both end up
With others (and I don't envy them!).

The mountain mourned the awful burden
Of a vow, too late to disavow.
The mountain murmured of the ancient tension,
That Gordian knot: of duty and of passion.

The mountain mourned our misery:
Tomorrow! Not right away! When our foreheads —
No longer bear the brand — quite simply — of
    death!
Tomorrow, when we understand.

A sound...as if someone, simply,
Well...was crying nearby?
The mountain mourned, we must go
Down, apart, through all that filth —

To life — we know all there is to know:
Rabble — market — barracks.
Still it murmured, all poems of mountains —
Are spelled out — *so*.

8.

Mount like a mound, hill like a hump
Of Atlas, groaning Titan.
A mound the toast of the town;
Sunup to sundown we

Shot the moon — like a game of hearts!
Passionate, we struggled *not to be!*
As you'd respect a bear trap,
Or the twelve apostles —

Honor my sullen cave!
(I was a cave, pierced by waves!)
Do you remember the last move
In that game — on the way out of town?

The mountain was — worlds!
The gods take vengeance on their likenesses!
. . . .
Misfortune had its origin on that mountain.
That mountain was — the tombstone on my grave.

9.

Years will pass. And look—
They will grind our graven mountain down to grave.
They will overwhelm our mountain with dachas,
They'll crowd it with a host of gardens.

They say out here, outside the city,
The air is pure, and life is easy,
So they'll begin to cut up little lots,
And dazzle with a thicket of new timbers,

To fence across my mountain passes,
And all my valleys—topsy-turvy!
For someone, somewhere has to be
At home in happiness, and bring *happiness* to the home!

Happiness—in the *home*! To love without fantasy,
Without bursting a vein.
You have to be a woman—and sustain!
(There was, there was, when you came around,

Happiness—in the home!) To love not cleaned up,
Not a separation, not like a knife.
On the ruins of our happiness
A town will rise: of husbands and wives.

And in that blessed air,
—While you are still able—sin!
There will be shopkeepers at leisure
To chew over profits,

To work out floor plans and entrances,
That every spare bit — find a home!
After all at least someone has to own
A house blessed by a stork!

10.

But under the weight of those foundations
The mountain will not forget — its little games.
They are wanton — they miss nothing:
The mountain has mountains — of time!

And along the stubborn faults the summer folk,
Reaching out too late, will seize:
Not the little hill, overgrown with families —
But a crater, stirred into a whirl!

You can't constrain Vesuvius — with vineyards!
You can't tie down a giant — with a thread!
Enough, the madness of *one single* voice,
That stirring, as a lion stirs,

The vineyards all begin to—come—undone,
Belching out a molten stream of hatred.
Your daughters will be harlots,
And poets, your sons!

You! Daughter! Whelp a bastard!
You! Son! Get into it with Gypsies!
Nor will you slake your thirst,
You mortals, on my blood!

Harder than a cornerstone, this curse,
Like a condemned man's deathbed oath:
Nor will you find terrestrial happiness,
You midges, on my mountain!

At an unknown moment, an unexpected time,
You all will recognize, as your entire tribe,
The exorbitant, the enormous mountain
Of the seventh commandment!

EPILOGUE

There are gaps in memory — cataracts
In the eyes: seven veils.
I can't picture you distinct from others.
In place of details — a white distress.

Without features. A pallid emptiness —
Complete. (The soul replete with wounds — just
One big wound.) To mark the cuts with chalk
Is for a tailor, or seamstress.

The firmament — is one whole heaven.
Is the ocean — just a crowd of waves?!
Without features. Everything — perfect — in its place.
Love is — connection, not dissection.

Raven-haired, or chestnut-maned? —
He has eyes to see: ask a neighbor.
Should passion take things into bits?
Am I a watchmaker, or doctor?

You're like a circle, whole and undivided:
A whirlwind *entire*, a *complete* paralysis.
And I can't think of you apart
From love. An exact equivalence.

(In heaps of dreamy down:
A waterfall, hills of foam —
A new thing, strange to the ear,
Instead of "I" — a royal "we..."]

But then, in this cramped and destitute
Existence: "Life as it is — and will be" —
I can't see you with another:
— Revenge of memory!

Prague, The Mountain
January 1–February 1, 1924

Poem of the End

I.

In a corrupt sky, rusted like tin,
A finger of a stake.
It rose at our appointed place
Like fate.

— "Quarter to? Correct?"
— Death doesn't linger.
Exaggerated, too tender,
The lift of his hat.

Challenge — in each eyelash.
Mouth pursed.
Extravagant, too low
The sweep of his bow.

— "Quarter to? Precisely?"
Voice lied.
Heart fell: what's with him?
Brain: a sign!

Sky of ill omens:
Tin and rust.
He waits at our accustomed place.
Time: six.

This soundless kiss:
Lip paralysis.
Just so — to the hand of a princess;
To the dead — like this.

Simple-folk jostling,
Elbows — in the side.
Too insistent, annoying,
Howl of a horn.

A howl — like a dog howls,
Goes on and on, goes mad.
(Too-muchness of life
At the time of death.)

Yesterday — waist-high,
Suddenly — to the sky,
(Enormous, there it lies:
Full size.)

In my head: sweet one, sweet.
— "The time? Past six."
— "To the movies, or...?" —
Explosion: Home!

2.

Gypsy fraternity —
Look where it led!
Like thunder overhead,
A brandished saber,

All the word-terrors
We knew would come,
A torn-down home —
That word: home.

◆ ◆ ◆

Spoiled whine
Of a lost child: home!
One-year-old kid:
"Give me!" and "Mine!"

My brother in dissipation,
My chill and fever,
Everyone else wants out,
But you? — To home!

◆ ◆ ◆

Like a horse at the hitching post — rearing
Head high! — and his lead in the dust.
— "But of course there's no home here!"
— "But there is, — ten steps further:

A home on the mountain."— "No higher?"
— "A home at the crest of the mountain."
The window under the very roof.
—*"And is it not on fire from*

The setting sun?" Just like, once again,
Life? Simplicity of a poem!
A home, which means, from home
Into night.
            (O, to whom will I tell

My sorrow, my trouble,
A horror, greener than ice...?)
— "You've been thinking much too much." —
A thoughtful: — "Yes."

3.

And now — the embankment. I cling
To the water, as if to a dense mass.
The hanging gardens of
Semiramis — just so!

Steely ribbon — of water,
A corpselike hue —
I cling, like a singer
To her score, like a blind man —

To the surface of a wall . . . No response?
Nothing? I lean toward you — are you listening?
I cling to all quenching thirst,
I cleave, like a sleepwalker

To the rim of a roof . . .
                    But this tremble
Is not from the river — naiad I was born!
To cling to the river, like a hand,
When my lover is at my side —

And faithful . . .
                    The dead are faithful,
Oh yes, but not to everyone, there in their tiny chambers . . .
Death on the left, and on my right side —
You. My right side like death.

Shaft of penetrating light.
Laughter, like a cheap tambourine.
— "You and I, together, should . . ."
(A shudder.)
— "Shall we be brave?"

4.

Wave of fair-haired
Fog — gauzy flounces.
Room full of breathing, smoking,
And the main thing — slandering!
What does it stink of? Of extra hurry,
Of indulgence and sin:
Of business secrets
And powdered noses.

Domestic bachelors
In their rings, overgrown boys...
Joking, laughing,
And the main thing — calculating!
Of large things and small,
Of snouts stuck with feathers.
...Of business bargains
And powdered noses.

(Half-turned: look, *here* —
Is *this* our house? — I'm mistress no longer!)
One — over his checkbook,
Another — over a kid-gloved little hand,
And that one — over a lacquered little leg
Works away quietly.
...Of business marriages
And powdered noses.

Silver notch in the window —
Star of Malta!
Fondling and petting,
And the main thing — squeezing!
Pinching...(Yesterday's viands —
Don't be too picky at the smell!)
...Of business trysts
And powdered noses.

The chain too short?
But then it's platinum, not steel!
Shaking triple chins, little calves —
They gobble veal.
On a sweet little neck
Skinny as a gas-lamp stem.
...Of business failures
And that explosive powder —
Of Berthold Schwartz...

                   he sure had
A gift — and helped out folks.
— "You and I need to talk."
Shall we be brave?

5.

I catch the quiver of a lip.
And I know: he won't speak first.
— "You don't love me?" — "No, I do."
— "You don't love me!" — "But I'm torn;

Wasted; worn."
(Like an eagle surveying the ground):
— "Forgive me, is *this* — a home?"
— "Home — is in my heart." —
                                        Stuff!

Love is flesh and blood.
A flower — that actually bleeds.
Do you think that love —
Is chatting across a little table?

An hour or so — and then for home?
Like these gentlemen and ladies?
So love, it means, . . .
— "A temple?"
O my child, you trade scar

For scar! — in full view of the servants
And the drunks? (And I, to myself:
"Love — is a bowstring
Under strain: a bow: a bowing out.")

— "So love is then — connection."
We're all in bits: life and lips.
(I begged you: don't put a spell on me!
That moment, secret, intimate,

That moment at the summit of the mountain
And of our passion. Memory — is like steam:
Love — is all good things thrown
In the fire — and always — for free!)

Shell-like slit of his mouth,
Pale. Not a smile — a calculation.
— "And most important, a single
Bed."
             — "You meant to talk

Of the abyss?" Drumbeat of fingers.
— "Let's not make mountains out of molehills!"
Love means...
                     — "Mine."
I understand you. And so?

◆   ◆   ◆

The drumming of fingers
Grows stronger. (Scaffold and square.)
— "We go." — And I, I was hoping,
We die. That would be simpler!

Enough of the cheap stuff:
Of rhymes, rails, hotel rooms, stations...
— "Love means: life."
— "No, it was called differently

By the ancients..."
                              — "And so?"
                                        Scrap
Of kerchief in the fist, like a fish.
"So let's go?" — "And your plan?"
Poison, rails, lead — yours to choose!

Death — without arrangements!
— Life! — A Roman general,
Reviewing his army like an eagle —
Those still standing.
                              — Then we'll say goodbye.

6.

— "I didn't want this.
No; not this." (Silently: listen!
Desire — that's for bodies,
And you and I — we're souls

From here on in...) — And he doesn't answer.
(And when the train is called
You offer your women, like a tumbler,
The wretched honor

Of the departure...) — "Am I dreaming?
Did I get this right?" (Civil liar,
Offering, like a flower,
The bloody honor of the rupture

To a lover...) — "Crystal clear: syllable
After syllable and then — goodbye?
Is that what you said?" (Like a kerchief
At the moment of sweet challenge

Dropped...) — "In this battle
You — are Caesar." (Insolent cut!
To hand back to an enemy
His surrendered sword —

Like a prize!) — He continues. (Ringing
In the ears...) — "I salute you, salute you:
It's the first time someone's beat me
To a parting." — This to all the girls?

Don't deny it! A vengeance
Worthy of Lovelace,
A gesture, you get honor,
I get flesh torn

From bone! — A snigger. In laughter,
Death. Gesture. (No desire.
Desire, that's a thing for — *them*,
And you and I? — shadows

From here on in...) He drives
A last nail. A last screw, coffin of lead.
— "One last request."
— "Go ahead." — "Don't breathe a word

Of us...not one...to anyone...well...
Of, you know, the next..." (So the wounded,
From their stretchers — in spring!)
— "I might ask you the same thing."

— "Can I give you a keepsake, a little ring?"
— "No." — His look, wide-eyed,
Is absent. (Like a seal
On your heart, like a ring

On your hand...without a scene!
We continue the drama.) More smoothly, softly:
— "Then a book?"
                    — "Like you give everyone?"
No, don't even write them,

Books...

◆ ◆ ◆

Must not
Must not
Must not cry.

Our wandering
Fraternities of fisherfolk
Dance — they don't cry.

They drink, but don't cry.
They spill hot blood —
They don't cry.

Melt tears — pearls
In a glass, and master
The world — they don't cry.

— "Can I go?" — I pierce him
With a glance. Harlequin, out of loyalty
To his Pierrette, as if tossing
A bone from his most despicable

Conquests: the honor of the end.
The bow at the curtain. The final
Speech. An inch of lead
In the chest: that would be better, hotter,

And — cleaner...
                    I bite
My lip with my teeth.
I will not cry.

Adamant of adamant —
Into softest flesh.
Just don't cry.

The wandering brotherhoods
Die, but don't cry,
They burn, but don't cry.

In ashes and in song
They hide the dead,
The wandering brotherhoods.

— "So you first? The first move?"
You mean, like chess? Why not?
After all, even on the scaffold
We women are first in line...
                                    Quick!

I beg you, don't look! — a glance —
(They're about to flood out in a torrent!
And how to stuff them back into
My eyes?!) — I say to you, you must

Not look!!!

Loud and clear,
A glance to the heights:
— "Sweet man, let's go,
Or I'll start to cry!"

I forgot! In the midst of walking
Piggybanks (You know — businessmen!)
His blond nape shone:
Maize; corn; rye!

All the commandments of Sinai
Washing away! — Maenad fur —
Golconda of hair,
Treasure house of pleasures —

(Promiscuous!) Nature doesn't gather
In vain, is not completely stingy.
From these blond tropics,
Hunters — how to

Get back? Teasing with coarse
Nakedness, and dazzling to tears —
The path is sodden with
Pure, golden, laughing adultery.

— "Isn't that true?" — A clinging, a grasping
Glance. In each eyelash — an itch.
— And the main thing — here in the lees!
A pattern, twisting in a braid.

O already the tearing of clothes!
Simpler than eating and drinking —
A smirk! (There's hope,
Alas, for your salvation!)

And — sisterwise or brotherwise?
Allies: a union!
— Not having buried you — to laugh!
(And having buried you — I'm laughing.)

7.

And now — the embankment. The last.
It's all over. Separate, without touching,
Like neighbors avoiding each other
We trudge along. From the bank of the river —

A weeping. I lick the fading, salty
Quicksilver without concern:
Heaven has not forbidden tears
To the enormous, Solomonic moon.

A post. Why not beat my forehead
Bloody? Not just bloody, to little bits!
Like frightened co-assassins we drag ourselves
Along. (The murdered thing — is love.)

Stop! Could this be two lovers?
Heading into night? Separately? To sleep with others?
— "Do you realize our future —
Is that?" — My head snaps back.

— "To sleep!" Like newlyweds on their mat...
— "To sleep!" We can never get in step,
In rhythm. Mournfully: "Take me by the arm!"
We're not convicts, nothing like that!...

A shock. (As if he touched me — on the arm
With his soul! — My arm with his arm.) The shock
Sears, like a charged wire
It tears — he touched my soul with his hand!

He clings. Iridescent, everything! What's more
    iridescent
Than tears? Like a curtain, more dense than beads,
The rain. — "I don't know if such embankments
Ever end." — A bridge, and: — "Then?"

Here? (Tumbrel supplied.)
Up . . . ward flutter of peaceful
Eyes. "Can we go home?"
For the very—last—time!

8.

The very—last bridge.
(Won't give you your arm; won't take back my own!)
The last bridge,
The last bridging.

The wa—ter is hard.
I count out my coins.
Day—wage for death,
Charon's bribe for Lethe.

Sha—dow of a coin
In a tenebrous hand. Soundless,
Mo—ney—for—these.
And so, in a tenebrous hand—

Sha—dow of a coin.
Without glint or clink.
Mo—ney—for—these.
The dead have enough poppies.

A bridge.

◆　◆　◆

To live — without hope
Is the fate of lovers:
Bridge, you are — like passion:
By convention, unbroken.

I nestle: warmth,
A rib — that's why I cling so.
No *pre-*, no *post-*:
An interval of insight!

No arm, no leg.
All bone and structure:
Alive only the side,
Which cleaves to the one beside me.

All life — to that side!
He is — ear, and he is — echo.
Like yoke to the white
I nestle, like a Samoyed to his fur

I cling, I nestle,
I dig in. Siamese twins,
What — your ally?
That woman — you remember: you called her

Mama? Forgetting
Everything, in frozen triumph,
Car—ry—ing you,
She did not hold you more dear.

Get this! We grew together!
We came true! You rocked to sleep on my chest!
I will not jump in!
To dive in, I'd have to

Let—go—your—arm. And I press close,
And I press close . . . And I'm not to be got rid of.
Bridge, you're no husband:
A lover — pure passing by!

Bridge, be for us!
We feed the river with bodies!
I swal—lowed you like ivy,
Like a tick: tear it out by the roots!

Like ivy! Like a tick!
Shamelessly! Inhumanly!
To—throw—me—away, like
A thing, not one thing

Not refuse in this
Material, hollow world!
Tell me this is a dream!
That it's night — and after night, morning,

On the ex—press train to Rome!
Or Grenada? Can't say, myself,
I've just brushed away cobwebs of
Mount Blanc and the Himalayas.

The opening is deep:
I warm you with the last of my blood.
Pay atten—tion to my side!
Is it not more true

Than po—et—ry? Does it not give heat?
And tomorrow, who'll pay your keep?
Tell—me this is delirium!
That there is not and never will be an end

To—this—bridge . . .
                        — but there is.

◆ ◆ ◆

— "Here?" A childlike, a godlike
Gesture. — "Well?" — I dig in, I grip.
— "There's still a tiny...tiny bit:
Until the last!"

9.

Like armies of factory workers, strident
And sympathetic to the summons . . .
That precious, sublingual secret
Wives keep from husbands, and widows

From friends — and for you, the inside information,
The secret Eve got from the tree — namely:
I'm no more than an animal
Wounded in the belly.

It burns . . . As if they'd stripped my soul
With my skin! Like steam from a spout,
That notorious heresy, preposterous,
The thing we call a soul.

Insipid Christian sickness!
Steam! To be cured with a salve!
There never was or will be such a thing!
There was a body, it wanted to live,

No longer.

◆ ◆ ◆

Forgive me! I take that back!
It was the howl of ripped intestine!
Just as, at four a.m.,
A condemned man awaits his execution

Playing chess, and taunting
The open corridor peephole with his grin.
After all, we're just pawns!
And someone plays with us.

Who? The kindly gods? Thieves?
Filling that peephole-like-an-eye —
An eye. From the red corridor,
A clank. The slide thrown back.

Drags on a cheap cigarette.
A hock — well, we've lived it up — another spit.
Across the checkered pavement
A straight path: to the ditch

And to blood. Secret eye:
Hidden wiretap of the moon...

◆ ◆ ◆

Cock of the head. A sideways glance.
— "You are already so far away!"

10.

A synchronous, a simultaneous
Startle — Our hangout!

Our island, our temple,
Where we, in the mornings —
Riffraff! A casual couple! —
Celebrated morning prayer.

Hubbub and buttermilk,
In half-sleep and spring...
The coffee was horrible —
Entirely of oats!

(They use oats to quiet
A headstrong horse!)
In no way of Arabia —
A scent of Arcadia,

That coffee...

But how she smiled at us,
Seating us side by side,
With the wise, compassionate,
Considerate smile

Of gray-haired lovers:
Live! You'll wither!
Smiled at madness, at poverty,
At boredom and at love, —

And the main thing — at youth!
At a laugh — without a reason,
At a smile — without consideration,
At a face — without creases —

O, the main thing — at youth!
At passions out of season!
Blown in from somewhere,
Washed in from somewhere,

Into the twilight of that milk bar:
— Tunis and burnoose! —
At hopes and muscles
Under the rot of chasubles ...

(Sweetheart, I'm not complaining:
Scar on scar!)
O, how she saw us off,
Our hostess in the

Pressed Dutch hat ...

◆　◆　◆

Struggling to remember, to understand all,
Exactly as if led from a celebration,
— "Our street!" — "No longer ours ..."
— "How many times ..." — "No longer *us* ..."

— "Tomorrow the sun will rise in the west!"
— "And David will break ranks with Jehovah!"
— "What are we doing?" — "We are separating."
— "That means nothing to me."

That extrasupermeaningless word:
Sep—a—rat—ing. Cal—i—brat—ing?
Simple word in four syllables,
Behind them, emptiness.

Wait! In Serbian and Croatian,
Maybe, but is the Czech acting up?
Sep—aration. To separate...
Extrasupermeaningless stuff!

A sound that bursts the ears,
Which stretch beyond the limit of sadness...
Separation — that's not Russian!
Not female speech! Not masculine!

Not God-speech! What are we — sheep,
Stifling great yawns at dinner?
Separation — what language is that?
Not even a scrap of sense,

Or even of sound! Well, just a hollow
Noise — of a saw, let's say, in a dream.
Separation — just the nightingale's moan,
From the school of Klebnikov,

Or a swan's...
                    And how does it escape?
Just like an empty reservoir —
Like air! Sound of arm against arm:
To separate — but of course that's thunder

Overhead...The sea's to our cabin!
The last ocean headland!
These streets — are too steep:
To separate — that means down,

Down the mountain...Sigh of two heavy
Boot soles...A palm, at last, and a nail!
Irresistible argument:
To separate — that means apart,

And we — are joined at the hip...

II.

To lose it all at one stroke —
There is nothing more clean!
Ex-urb, sub-urb:
End of days.

Of comforts (read — of stones),
Of days, of us, of homes.

Dachas standing empty! Like an ancient
Mother — I honor them both the same.
That's at least an action — to be empty.
What's hollow can't be empty.

(But dachas emptied by a third?:
Better to go up in flames!)

Only don't be shocked
When you rip open a wound.
Ex-urb, sub-urb,
Split out a stich!

For — without pompous, without superfluous
Language — love is a seam.

A seam, but not a sling; a suture — not a shield.
— O, don't ask for protections! —
A seam that sews a dead man to the earth,
That fixes me to you.

(And time will tell how well:
Just basted, or with a triple stitch!)

Somehow or other, friend — along the seams:
Scraps and rags!
The only good thing is it burst:
Burst, did not just rot away.

And under the seam, a living vein,
Pink and sound — and not decay!

O, he's not losing this on a toss,
He's tearing this to bits!
Ex-urb, sub-urb,
Forehead split!

They do to death in the villages, now —
Cold wind in the brain!

O, he's not gambling this away, who's off —
At the hour when dawn catches fire.
I sewed a whole life for you at night,
Complete, finished, without correction.

So don't reproach me, if it doesn't please...
Suburb, torn seams.

Souls, their stitches
In a mess!...
Ex-urb, sub-urb,
The fierce extent

Of the suburb. Do you hear
The jackboot of fate — in the sloppy clay?
...Think of my quick work,
My friend, and this hurried, tenacious

Thread — like it, don't give way!
The very—last streetlight!

◆ ◆ ◆

Here? As if casting a spell —
A look. Of the worst kind. —
A look.
        — "Can we go to the mountain?"
For the very—last—time!

12.

Rain, a thick mane
In the eye. — Hills.
We have escaped the suburb.
We are outside the city.

There exists — but only for others —
A stepmother - - not a mother!
This is as far as we go.
To die here, to be put down.

A field. A fence.
Brother and sister we stand.
Life is a suburb! —
Build outside the city!

Ay, the game
Is up, my friend!
Everything — suburbs!
Where are the cities?!

It tears at us and rages,
The rain. We tear each other and rage.
First thing we've done together
In three months!

And from Job, Lord,
Did you look for a loan?
That didn't work out, did it:
We're beyond the city!

❖ ❖ ❖

Beyond the city! Get it? Beyond!
Outside! We've crossed the embankment!
Life — is where it's forbidden to live:
The Jew—ish quarter...

Is it not a hundred times more worthy
To die as the Wandering Jew?
Because if you're not a warrior, a son of Gad,
A Jew—ish pogrom —

Is what life is. To live is only for converts!
For the Judases of all the faiths!
Off to the leprous isles!
To hell! — To anywhere! — But not

To life, — which only tolerates converts,
Only lambs — for the slaughter!
I hand back my right-to-live-here,
I—stamp—it underfoot!

I trample it! For the shield of David,
Payback! — In a stack of bodies!
And is it not fantastic
A Jew lives — and didn't want it?!

Chosen-ness of the ghetto! Dike and ditch.
Expect no mercy!
In this most Christian of worlds,
Poets — are Jews!

13.

Just as they sharpen knives on stone,
Just as they whisk away the filings.
Beneath my hands something
Moist, something soft and warm.

Where are you, you twin virtues:
Manly power, self restraint?
Beneath my palm —
Tears, not rain!

What desires still merit
Speech? All I own — dissolves!
Since your diamond eyes
Shed tears beneath my palm —

I lack nothing.
The end of the end!
I stroke — I stroke —
I stroke your face.

Such is our arrogance —
Us Marinas, us Poles.
After your eagle eyes
Have wept beneath my palm...

Are you crying? My friend!
My everything! Forgive me!
But how coarse, salt
In the hollow of my hand!

A husband lets slip a cruel tear:
Like a cudgel to the head!
Cry! You will redeem this shame
With others, you are at sea with me.

From an iden—tical
Ocean — fish!
A salute — like a dead shell,
Lips to lips.

◆　◆　◆

In tears.
Astringent —
Bitter.
— "And when
I wake up
Tomorrow?"

14.

A sheep path —
This descent. Sound of the town.
Three girls going our way.
They are laughing. They laugh

At the tears, — like full noon
Of the underworld, the crest of the wave!
They laugh! — at the
Improper, shameful,

Tears of a man, seen
Through the rain — in two slashes!
Like a pearl — disgraceful
On a soldier's bronze.

At your first tears,
And your last — O pour them out! —
At your tears — pearls
In my crown!

Of course I don't look down.
Through the downpour — I stare back.
Little love dolls,
Look your fill! This union

Is more intimate
Than the act of love.
The very Song of Songs
Makes way for our words,

Solomon bows down before us:
These little, unknown birds —
Because our mingled weeping —
Is greater than a dream!

◆ ◆ ◆

And in the hollow of a wave
Of darkness — grieved and in equipoise —
Without a trace — without a sound —
A ship — goes down.

Prague, February 1–
Jíloviště, June 8, 1924